The Patient

George MacBeth

Hutchinson
London

© The Estate of George MacBeth 1992

This edition first published in 1992 by
Hutchinson

Random House UK Limited
20 Vauxhall Bridge Road, London SW1V 2SA

Random House Australia (Pty) Ltd
20 Alfred Street, Milsons Point, Sydney, NSW 2061, Australia

Random House New Zealand Ltd
18 Poland Road, Glenfield, Auckland, New Zealand

Random House South Africa (Pty) Ltd
PO Box 337, Bergvlei, 2012, South Africa

A CIP catalogue record for this book is available from the British
Library.

ISBN 0 09 177543 4

Set in Ehrhardt by Edna A Moore, ⅍ Tek-Art, Addiscombe,
Croydon, Surrey
Printed and bound in Great Britain by Cox and Wyman Ltd,
Reading

To my friends at the
Kings Lynn Poetry Festival

Contents

A Conversation
for the Nineties

HUSBAND:

If I were a warrior
And not weak, as I am,
I would slaughter an adventurer
Who came for your child, or your life.
I would roast his bones
For your dinner.

Why, therefore,
When I am consumed
By a discriminating appetite,
Will you not freely
Open the hairy gates of your belly
To my probing?

WIFE:

Because I, too, am weak,
An exchange of services
Is only possible between the hungry.
If I desired
Your steaming thickness
Up to its root in my body

I would hire a machine-pistol
And slaughter an adventurer
Who came for your child, or your life.
I would poach his testicles
For your breakfast.
So there.

ADVENTURER:

I am an adventurer
With a red-hot poker
Up my bottom.
Intercourse can be nasty, too.
I recommend that you both
Become vegetarians, and celibate.

This is not a time
To make a powerful enemy.
The devil is out, looking
For astray sexual organs
To make a stew for his dog.

So beware.

To My Old Typewriter

L. C. Smith, 1918

You cost me five pounds in an Aylsham sale.
For over a decade you've served me well
And it's not your fault, if I have to stop.
My fingers won't divide; you're out of luck.
What earlier owners may have punched your keys
I've never known. I don't suppose I've cared.
For you were the nanny of my prime

And raised seven novels on your roller bar
And sent five books of poems ribboning
Through many drafts. You might send many more,
But not for me. I ask you to lie fallow
Across my office in memoriam
Of our twelve years together, yoked as one.
A willing workhorse at the study fire

You always waited, saddled up, ready to go
Over the fences when I caught the scent
Of a foxy piece of prose, or a foxy poem.
Yield to the tractor now. Your electric cousin
Plugged in the wall is all that I can manage.
Others may come one day, when I am dead,
And buy you cheaply, and perhaps treat you right

And give more business to your solid frame.
I hope so. As I touch your shift in sadness
I feel a tremor as of something moving
Anxious to work again, and be of use.
Lie still in dust. The time for iron will come.
The day of brass and modest wood will come.
An honest few will always honour you.

Herky

Down by the bog, and the bog water,
The dog fell. He had come a long way

Out of the encampment, towards the Big House
When the girl found him, shivering on the steps,
And took him in. It was mid July
But cold for the season. His fur was matted,
The way a favourite toy's is matted
And she combed him through. Herky, she murmured,
Remembering a friend from long ago,
And Herky is who he became, no longer nameless

But the rightful heir to a great property
Haunted by the fairies. The dead Hercules
Barked later, after the Great War,
When her son came home. So much was dark
In those days. Even the blaze in the grate
Held secrets beyond our power to reckon.

Burning turf, hauled from the bog
Where the heir laboured, troubled the air.

The Price

Knowing that you are coming, and quite soon,
I sense the glory of the world unchanged.
The sun keeps rising. Sometimes even the moon
Comes up as if a birth has been arranged.

It has. Not more than seven months away,
You wave to me across the skinny hill
Where, bean-like, you grow strong. What must we pay
For something so conducive to good will?

Is there a price for what the cold stars bring
And lay in screaming wonder at our feet?
Some barter for our unformed gathering
That grows to raw flesh in the womb's white heat?

I think there is. An invoice for our joy
Whether you be my daughter, or a boy.

The Sick

The sick are like the old. When muscles waste
They end as famished shadows of themselves.
Their skin goes cold, the colour of the paste
That seventies put on to look like twelves.

A second childhood comes. And then a third.
Steel wheel-chairs carry babies to their meals
Where eating means extrusion of a turd.
The costive athlete squirms on useless heels.

Imagine, then, the evening traffic jams
These dream of, where they idle, browse and talk,
The stirrup-cups they manage, the young lambs
They seem like when their mounted bodies walk.

Yes, walk. Some dream they walk again through a door,
Even dance a fox-trot on a slippery floor . . .

The Sick Husband

I worry sometimes that you might go mad
When you wake up, and feel my wasted hands.
It makes me angry, then it makes me sad,
Manacled – like a convict in iron bands.

Your kindness hates these gnarled hands that it calms.
It suffers them and shivers. If I can,
And I can't often, I withdraw my palms
And quit your breasts. You love another man,

The one I was. I lift myself and smile,
And rub your back with fingers that feel strong
And talk about the baby. Sometimes I'll
Say something stupid, and you'll take it wrong.

Then we both feel the ache from being one.
Love isn't always a whole lot of fun.

The Healthy Wife

I think I'd die but for our separate rooms.
We miss each other, yes. But that can help.
Illness can be presumptuous. It consumes
It leaves you beached on care like stranded kelp.

We eat each other with our winsome eyes,
Then grow through severance towards normal chores.
You try, with difficulty, to zip flies
And grope for light switches; toe open doors.

Often I dream that, in a space of time,
It'll plateau out, a magic cure will come.
I scrape through magazines, a sexual mime.
Helping to ease the tensions in my bum.

Later there'll be real sex, an interim.
Then back to separate rooms. Life's pretty grim.

The Sick Driver

Driving home through the worst of the year,
You splash up water, suck on lemon drops.
The windscreen's blurred with teardrops and won't clear.
Outside, the rain lams down. It never stops.

Tiring, you stray towards other lanes,
Then nod off, and your braking foot's in glue.
Energy, focussed on a green sign, drains,
And then your muscle's moving, and you're through.

With someone else it might be accident,
With you it's consequence of your disease.
Whatever happens has to have been meant,
And be a symptom. So don't start to creep

Towards the kerb. You have to stay awake.
You blink your eyes. You slow for safety's sake.

At Home

Tomorrow, they decided. He would go
In his wheel-chair to St Sebastian's
And check the costs. Charges might be quite low
For a mobile case. Well, homes may have their fans

But he's not one of them. No, he'll not roll
Through pearly gates to play the dying game.
He'd rather shiver at the stark North Pole
Of an ingratitude that knows no shame.

They laughed then. Rhetoric undid the strings
And laid them hugging in each other's arms.
But grief brings witnesses. She spreads her wings
And trouble had her echoing alarms

Far below kisses, below intercourse.
The need for change was gathering its force.

Homes

You've seen them often, classical affairs
With porticoes and porches, grey and gaunt.
The inmates are – outside. In basket chairs
They're wheeled to take the sun, a kind of taunt.

Their future dwindles into fields of sheep
Under a sky of settling rain, then snow.
What gave them pleasure most returns in sleep
And warms their tongues, from churns of long ago.

Their palsied hands are shrunk. Their eyes implore
The blank horizon and the passing cows.
Pain infiltrates their bodies floor by floor.
Their brains are mortuary rooms that house

The corpses of what was, and what will be.
Then someone brings a trolley with their tea.

Wife's Needs

Courage is nothing. It's not being brave
That helps. They don't see that at all.
It's humour, laughing. When you feel the slave
Of someone too demanding, tasks appal

That otherwise don't matter. Making light
Of things, not asking, waiting, smiles.
Those are four dos for invalids. Be polite,
Say thank you, tell some jokes. All this beguiles.

I know you're sick. It makes me scream with pain
Remembering the way you were and are.
But I don't want you to show it. Let the reign
Of shared appliances begin, the car

Be mine to drive, your laughter shine through hell.
Then we can stay together fairly well.

The Worst Fear

Some days I do feel better. Then I know
It couldn't come to this, it never would.
I'm much the same as I was long ago
When I could walk two thousand yards, and stand

Upright at parties, chatting. When the men
At petrol stations understood
The words I mouthed. Now is the same as then.
It isn't, though. These are the days when food

Falls from my grip, drink chokes me in my throat
And I'm a nervous nuisance, prone to tears.
The time has come when I put on my coat
With fumbling fingers, grappling with my fears

Of God knows what. Well, I know one that's worse
Than all the rest. My wife's become my nurse.

Jack

Others are worse, of course. Jack hisses by
Blank-eyed in his thick-rubber-tyred car.
In seven months he knows he's going to die,
Or thinks he is. His death is like a star

He sees at night go whistling up the sky
To whet a scythe, a sort of sharpening-blade.
All flesh is grass and his is shortening rye.
We get the point; hour after hour we wade

Up to our necks in far worse puns than this.
The automatic wheel-chair does its turn
Down corridors where corners meet and kiss
And under windows where light curtains burn.

Some of us laugh. Some of us take the strain.
For Jack the fuse is lit and burning in his brain.

A Piss Artist

A Dialogue

'Yesterday something happened at ten to three.'
'Tell us about it.' 'Well, his prick got trapped
Inside his trousers, and he couldn't pee,
And then he could, and then he nearly crapped.'

'A good job that he didn't, I suppose
And put your poem really in the shit
Instead of shivering like seamless prose
With only urine flowing over it.'

'Don't I deserve it? Wouldn't anyone,
Wouldn't you say, who can't control his water
And has to dry his jodhpurs in the sun
Or wear a nappy like his baby daughter?'

'You don't find that too funny.' 'Nor do I
With soaking underpants behind my fly.'

The Young Nurse

One of the nurses told him off today
For fiddling with his willy. (But he can't.)
She came in carrying a wooden tray,
His eggs and bacon, at an awkward slant,

Then tripped and nearly fell. 'You dirty beggar,'
She smiled and said, 'you'll soon exhaust your strength
If you keep straining on.' He'd like to peg her
Down on the floor, and straddle her full length.

(But he can't.) Farewell, sex, from these verses.
You could come back if he could masturbate.
He'd do it in the bath, and bellow curses,
Then wipe his belly like a child's black slate.

Meanwhile, he mouths his breakfast by the fire,
Wishing that nurses' fingers were for hire.

Reading Matter

A touch of Larkin, and a stroke of pain.
A trace of Henley, and a smear of grief.
The fearful stick to Alistair Maclean,
A book on spiders, or the Barrier Reef.

The brave attempt the Bible, or some Freud,
Analyses of madness and of death
And afterlife projections as the void.
Not many, though, are fit for late MacBeth

And his doom-laden scenes, predestined woe.
Most prefer television, world news
From somewhere everyone would like to know
After a convalescing luxury cruise:

Hawaii, the Bahamas, Tenerife.
Autumn, though, goes on falling, sere leaf by leaf.

The Confinement

I thought about the dwarf, Toulouse-Lautrec
Who lived with whores, and had his way with whores.
It wasn't just a kiss and then a neck.
He screwed them, and he gave them sores

That he'd inherited from other whores.
Life might be a confinement, you a wreck,
But why not satisfying? Why with bores?
Why live in some dull home, and drown in dreck?

Wasn't it better with the prostitutes
In a Victorian brothel, gold and red,
Where men came in to fuck in business suits
And no-one ever thought about being dead?

I wonder. It's the best at home in bed,
I think, arranged like spoons, my cheek against your head.

A Miracle

Lee-Hamilton got better. An Ironside,
Hysterically ill, for half a life
He was a stretcher case, damn nearly died.
Then he rose up like Lazarus. A wife

Lifted his spirits, and they had a child.
Lucky Lee-Hamilton, you say. But why,
What cured him? It seems no-one filed
A diagnosis, it's a mystery.

Of course, he got some good reviews at last
After his 'Sonnets of the Wingless Hours'.
Was that his cure, my message from the past,
That I can excavate unearthly powers?

But where's that miracle, the good review
Able to mend dead nerves? I haven't a clue.

The Consultant

He writes, and that's a victory of a kind.
I don't read poetry, and I can't scan verse,
But there's no adverse action on his mind.
Oh no. Take Stephen Hawking, he's much worse,

But he can lecture with a borrowed voice,
Commutes through Cambridge streets, and, well, his books
Outsell the lot of them. If there's no choice
About the muscle wasting, it still looks

As if the benefit may be a gain
In intellectual fervour. What creates
Preserves a power to be crazy plain
And piles up energy like cakes on plates.

He's highly motivated. Not like Jack.
Oh, yes, he'll survive a while. But he'll be back.

The Mirror

I watch an old man with a knotted, flamboyant tie
Walking on two sticks up the road. He looks
About twenty years older than me, very nearly eighty.

Sometimes he stops for a rest, stares up at the windows
Where younger people are laughing, blowing kisses to each
other.
Sometimes he smiles, as if at a private joke.

I like this old man. I admire his slow progress
Towards an inevitable pause, perhaps for a drink.
I smile, and he smiles back. Life's funny, really.

There are days, though, when I can't match his aplomb.
I glare at the mirror. I want the glass to break
And let the young man out, who is inside, crying.

Shotts

Grown-over slagheaps rise like burial mounds
For giant moles: the outworks of a siege
Where coal that ruled their lives fell back and failed.

Subsidence, unturned wheels. Fresh conifers
In tiny forests mark the perished seams
And ragwort flares above blown galleries.

Where shafts go down, there must lie bones of men
And dregs of anthracite, once linked by work
As at the brink of something, luck or change.

I see my father, measuring his hat
Against my little skull, day after day
Go down those shafts and frame a better future.

I was born here. Now, after sixty years,
I come back weaker to the place of launching
And drive through dirty streets, tears in my eyes.

Strawberry Fields

We drove in the car towards the strawberry fields
Where the others picked. I sat and waited,
Immobile as a one-year-old in my seat-belt
Under the shadow of the Malvern Hills,
The ducal leaves, and eye-wet berries.

Nothing much there for a poem. But I wanted
More than I showed to make some contribution
To the feast of the world. I owed a return
For what was given through the eyes once
And upon the hands, legs moving

Towards fulfilment. So I wrote and celebrated
Sweetness and greenfly
Not seeing or feeling, but sensing still
In the red flood of imagination
All that they meant, and were.

I picked, too. I came home in the car
With my own gathering,
A punnet of berries, wet with dew,
Torn from the scratching shrubberies
Of desire and failure.

Bite the dark flesh
Of the never-forgotten fruit
And sink your tongue in the tart softness.
These are the paper heirs,
The beaded relics fresh still from the branches.

The Patients

There are five patients I have to tell you about.
Michael first, with his nid-nodding head
And his love of Christian names, Jason from Bedford
Who has twenty seconds' warning
Before his attacks – time to stop the car –
　　And Roger who never smiles.

I mean, if you were Roger, penned in a chair
At the age of thirty-two, I wonder
If you would smile? Peter thinks not,
Painting the agile young Indian from Brixton
With his left hand, the only part
　　Not affected by his disease.

'Do you still have erections?' they ask,
That 'still' hovering like the blade
Of the guillotine. Doctors are mean,
Mustapha thinks, whom they ask often
While they toy with the pit of his arm.
　　An operation perhaps

Will carry Mustapha past forty. There remains
Colder comfort for the others. At home now
Soldiering on with my limp and my cough
I remember Michael and Jason, Roger and Peter
　　And Mustapha,

Those foot soldiers in the long retreat
From the Moscow of getting well
　　And I say a prayer:

Dear God, who created the human condition
And put the pain and death in the bottle,
Let there be scotch and water for those poor sinners
Who have no more hope, and a shot of morphine
　　To carry them through.

The Man Who Wanted to See the Flowers

It wasn't that he was blind, or paralysed.
He could have got down there on someone's arm,
Angling past the manky cat and the tennis court.
He could have been propped on a window-sill
And broken off some stalks of larkspur.

But for what? A lot of bother
To someone who wasn't interested
In the exercise routines of the humble
Who count a few strides as a miracle.
It wasn't worth it really. So he didn't go.

He sat upstairs in the window-alcove
Under a great arch of eighteenth-century glass
And admired the poppies, from a distance. And the mock
                                        orange
And the billiard-table look of the mown lawn.
You see, he was rich. He had everything that he wanted.

They brought him new-blown roses, put them in a vase
Where he would pass them every day
On his way to shave. He could still do this,
He was lucky. He leaned on a dado rail
And bent his nose to those indoor, dying roses.

He was lucky. There were children in deserts
Who had never smelled a dying rose
Because they were more interested in the odour of food,
It came so rarely. The man knew this
Like he knew his own name. So why did he sit

Staring down at the not quite inaccessible garden
With that look in his eyes? We know the answer
The way we know the size of a stone
Or the weight of a bird. How what remains in reach
But is slipping away matters more than a jewel.

The hungry cry for what they have never known,
Or knew once, and may have again.
Sustenance, the bliss of renewal. But the failing
Watch the ferry leaving the quay,
And the gap widening, and know they can never jump.

Laughter in Hell

I'm a baby
Growing backwards. Every day
  A little bit less. Can't walk
  So many yards. Harder to pour the tea.
Phlegm in the throat. I have a bath
With qualms. Approach bumpy ground
  Leaning on someone's arm. Type
  With a lot of difficulty. Writing a cheque
When it's cold can take a long time. Why cold?
I don't know. There's a lot they don't know
  About life. But I'll tell you one thing.
  It's a lethal, progressive, incurable
Disease. Like mine.

Thus the man on splints, gritting his teeth
  As he fell on the terrace.
  But they came soon,
Bearing toast, a fur hippopotamus,
The new *Poetry Review*, anything.
  Anything at all
To block the bones in his hands,
The skeleton below the skin
Sneering at them. Old friends were worst
  With their frightening sympathy

Instead of news. What's the prognosis?
He's walking slower
Than last year. It must be terrible for you.

So make a joke,
Maybe take him away for a while. I can read
    The tea-leaves for myself.
Some days he's fine, yes. I don't know, no.
I don't know what I'll do
    If he gets worse. I mean when, yes.
One fucker was even crying. I'll do the crying,
Sonny boy, you stand and listen. Give
    Me a break. Friends!
I'd rather have enemies,
They make me try harder. What's that?
    There's no pain.
He just gets very tired. He can hardly stand sometimes

Imagine buttons
That won't go into their holes. Shoelaces
    You can't untie. Fancy going to bed
    In your brogues? And a zip
You need two hands for. A scenario.
The man stumps into a lavatory
    On his dog-headed stick. Leans the stick
In a corner. Leans on the wall
With one hand, and fumbles. Meanwhile, the piss,
    Growing tired of waiting, comes
With a gush. Over the seat,
Over the whole world
    It sometimes seems. And he has to wipe it up.

There are nights
When I think of euthanasia. Nights
   When I watch television, dreaming
   Of running for a bus again. Nights
When it all seems just like yesterday, except
   For the stiffness in my joints. Roll on,
   Cataclysm. Let someone else have it.
Lung cancer, blow up in Armagh, lose his daughter
In a car crash. Join the club.
   I'm sick of being alone
   In the wheel-chair dream.
The brakes fail. You can't get away
   From the mugger. I have to stand or choke.

It dissolves, though. There are mornings
When I wake fairly cheerful. I rise
   And manage to shave. Not so bad.
I look out and it's raining. The cows
Don't look so good either. I get downstairs,
   Eat some breakfast. I read a book
Or the papers. Maybe they'll find a cure. Pigs
   Might fly. Ironic laughter
   Can make you choke on a blood pressure pill.
It's a joke. There's no pain,
So you can't be ill. I laugh, I go
   On laughing. Remember, you laugh
And the world laughs with you. Laughter in paradise.
                          Laughter in hell.

The Man in the Iron Lung

Suppose the amount of cash available
Became a synonym for the years you had to live,
It wouldn't any longer be a question of Peter Porter's
'Why do they worry about money who are shortly going to
die?'

The two things would be one and the same.

Which is why men with salaries
Manage better than those retired, or free-lances.

It helps to have stuff coming in, prolonging time,
An intake of what's necessary,
Like breathing.

Otherwise, you fret about cheques
Restricted wedding-presents
Becoming a hard-won holiday
From the sense of going downhill fast.

A miser,
Trying to expand the capital
In your treasure-chest.

Life is a Progressive Disease

The invaluable lies:

You're walking better, best
Thing you've ever written, I
Love you.

Smugglers

The roads of your empire are black-topped and level
And her poets are Walcott and Shapcott and Wevill.

Outside in the darkness we long for the price
Of her petrol and liquor, her bread and her rice.

The empire has jobs and the empire has flowers
And elegant National Trust-maintained towers.

But we think of her soldiers shot up in the air
And we'd rather be here than demoralised there.

The empire is rich and her colours are red
But too many of those who defend her end dead.

Out here in the darkness our colours are green
And we stare at our films on an old, grainy screen.

We thrive on the dole and we fiddle for our supper
And some of us live on no more than a cuppa.

But others drink Guinness, and some even Paddy's,
And these are the dangerous, braw-lidded laddies

Who drive to the border and lay out their planks
And bring home your goods for Sweet Afton and thanks.

The goods, are they bottles, or do I mean guns,
The Armalite rifle, the grenade that stuns?

O down here we're solid, with drinks on the slates,
And our poets are Durcan, Kavanagh and Yeats.

The Patient

Alive in the torture-chamber,
He stared at the flowers: the scent of freesia
Like a nerve gas, even the teddy bears
On his get-well card were leering.

It had been a fun week.
His head offered the claustrophobia of a box
And a pair of magnets, electrodes
Clamped to his wrists and ankles.

Rumour had it
They put the current through your balls
If you mentioned impotence.

Meanwhile, the doctors
Went round and round like clockwork,
Like the grand alliance against the Iraqis,
In the sand.

He refused the hara-kiri of a milligram,
Took the short cut to his death sentence,
And ate his dinner.

A Loss of Power

In 1976,
The lights went out in New York City
For nearly twenty-four hours.

There were cardiac arrests on stairs
When the lifts failed,
Lots of looting.

Then the lights came on again,
Things got better.

But not for me.
They took the muscles out of my toes,
The grip from my right hand.

I'm afraid of a boy
With a television set
Running out of my throat.

Physio-therapy

A pretty girl limped in.
She lay down on her back
On the bed,
Wearing tights and a tank top.
She lifted her knees.

A second girl bent down between the first girl's knees,
Heels under her bottom.
She put her palms inside the first girl's thighs.

'Try to stop me opening your legs,' she said.

But the first girl couldn't, however much
She strained and cried.

All the men in wheel-chairs
Found it very erotic.

Thoughts of the Muscle-man or Feeling His Lost Biceps

It takes thirty-one candles to
Light my drawing-room,
But I can see to read by one.

In 1950,
A week's butter ration was two ounces.
Today I need more than a pound and a half.

So what's new with the power crisis?

The Blizzard

The last battle
Of walking a few strides uphill in Worcester
Terminated his enthusiasm for exercise.

Thousands of blood-cells
Died in their bunkers.

Meanwhile,
Snow fell over minarets
Where the faithful
Abused their commentators, able
For more. About himself,
He was never sure.

The bombardment never stops
In your nerves. You go on
As if into a blizzard
Where luck is invisible.

Islamic Affair

A disorganised, sick and undependable army
Was standing still, feet in the mud,
They would capture Babylon quite easily,
Even Persepolis, but after that?

The army stirred in its size ten boots, dreading bull.

Meanwhile, the enemy, from their minarets
Looked down and spat,
Waiting for an engagement, which might never take place.

Crows

At night the crows came back
Out of the fields
Where they ate his blood.

They slept in his brain.

In the morning, one crow would go. Then the others
Like a flight of bombers
Left him, for ever.

What they devoured would never return.
He could only dream of crows.

Bad News

The blast of a shotgun will get you nowhere.
Nowhere at all.

The driver of a truck facing me faces nowhere.
Nowhere at all.

In the skull of my gun
The impermanence of his future
Resolves itself to a shadow.

The gun thinks, it senses the horror of this.
It feels like a shit, ejecting cartridges.

But it rules the world,
Crooked lines on blotting paper
Where the figures dance to attention,
Men and women
With little brains in their fearful genitals.

The same goes for bad news.
It blows a hole in the head
The size of an earthquake.

Through this the magnificent paraphernalia
Of wisdom enters.

A pantechnicon of surprises.

Biting its own tail, like a scorpion in a ring of fire.

Trials of a Partner

Watching him fall gave her a strange feeling,
Like sex, without love.

Again and again,
She plugged in to the baby
But its message was only milk.

Silk
Lined the wall of her womb
Where they fucked, in lethal silence.

All those nasty mysteries in the bones of tomorrow
Signalled and stuck.

Sorrow, they say,
Is a kind of paracetamol for the gentle.
It dulls their pain.

But the strain
Of being Mrs Nice Guy
Was too much for Pandora. She opened the box

In her bowels
And a knife flew up
Into the heart of the matter.

Idle chatter
Will get you nowhere. He has to die
Sooner than planned; and, as if trepanned,

A slice of her brain fell out
Like a golden cornice
And broke on the floor, where he crawled.

The Thinking Doctor

Inside the thinking doctor's head
The people started to be dead.

One by one, through gaseous air,
They fell in Revolution Square.

One breathed his last and shouted 'Water!'
They only brought him further slaughter.

But oil was what they did it for,
Dragged their asses up the shore

And fucked the shit from Sad Hussein
Who breathed his last in muddy rain.

Later, those who'd lost their legs
And walked on sticks like shell-less eggs

Wondered if that oil was worth
A sacrifice of so much earth

Iraq and Jordan spoiled for years
And Latvia in grease and tears –

Grease and tears and blood and money.
The thinking doctor found that funny.

Putting away his stethoscope
He crushed the final ant of hope.

'You choose paralysis or mania
In Galway or in Lithuania.'

Legs

Rested up, during the Depression.

Came out on a de la Salle,
And blew the hand off a man, in des Moines.

The man was me.

Lying a little, for the sake of appearances,
And not any more in the numbers racket
Or able to shoot the pips
From the ace of spades.

Dying early, gone west,
Like all the rest of the kids.

The bitches, the bastards. The gangsters.

That's me there in the picture, beside Legs Diamond.

Lines for a Cataclysm

Now for a comment
From the breeders of stuck pigs
In Curaçao, the monitors

Who watch the progress of incunabula
Selling at par. Whodunits
Give off a low steam

Attractive to the black marketeers.
Too late. Forgive me.
We are going under

All together, singing 'God Save the Queen'
With the volume turned down
So as not to wake the children.

Long live the republic of ridicule,
The men who can walk,
The little girls who will one day stand on their own feet.

Casualty List

He comes in for the tests.

Meanwhile, the men in gaiters
Go about their business, unpremeditated. The wrung hands
And the pouting buttocks accost their divinities

Lord have mercy. Allah be praised.

The braised
Steak of the bodies accumulates. In one fireball
A crew takes the lift to Heaven, a missile
Judges its own distance to nowhere. Men
Obstruct and connive.

We remain alive
By virtue of the frail travelling coincidence
Known as error.

Terror
Shines in the dials. Green as gangrene,
A new story begins:

Casualty list.

The last flicker of an eyelid.

To the Former Ladies of My Acquaintance

Ladies, I hardly dare to name
So many whom I may have known
But still am friends with, all the same.
Your dog now offers you a bone
To pick with him, which may atone
For what was once a mort of cares.
I led you all a dance, I own,
And now retire more slow upstairs
Fencing my way through falling shares.
Promote my pages to your hearts
Where I may lie with bulls and bears
And think no more of strawberry tarts
Than I have done of truth and lies
In writing down these mysteries.

Falls Road

Was where you fell.

It wasn't only if you were a Catholic.

You fell in the hall, too, on the stairs,
And once in the field.

And once in front of the television set,
Prostrating yourself
As if towards Mecca.

Watching the news about Saddam Hussein
And his crimes.

In all, you fell about fourteen times.

You fell in the Bank
And were picked up by a cashier.
Now tell me girls, how many of you
Have been picked up by a cashier?

You were picked up by a policeman, too.
Outside a public lavatory.

Your knees bruised, and a mark on your arm
Like the Dome of the Rock.

You fell so often,
You started to call the world Falls Road
Because it was there
You always hurt yourself, although you survived.

You fell in a bookshop once, where they knew who you
were,

And that was the worst.

It wasn't the first, and it won't be the last.

When you start to fall,
It sometimes goes on quite a long time.

Epitaph for a Suicide

He remembered a gas-mask
That had lost its mother.

He heard the shrapnel squeal,
All the way to market.

Nobody cared. Nobody cares now, he thought,
As he lifted a dog-headed stick
In his wasted hand
And shook it at silence.

Egyptian gods came out of the woodwork
And squinted through him. But he paid no attention.

The wag-clock was ticking
Like a table-shelter. There had to be bombs,

For there to be peace. That was the principle
Most of us live by.

But the rest die, only slowly.

So he took up the hour-glass
Like a cyanide capsule
And crushed it between his teeth.

Crying wolf, once too often.

To My Old and Loyal Friend, Anthony Thwaite, Esq.

Anthony, you're a loyal friend
And one I've known for many years.
As we approach the century's end,
Saluting you with friendly tears
Under the dying chandeliers,
I ask you for some sound advice.
Give me some message for my ears
And let it not be imprecise
About the virtues and the vice
Of what I offer as a book
Expected to secure a price.
Will any reader take a look
Or is it hardly worth the time
Of someone with a taste for rhyme?

Prologue

If I supposed you needed this
Or anything so mad and small
I might have let my serpent hiss
Before I scotched him once for all.
But I have grown too wise and tall
To bother with such empty things
As knights and ladies and the Fall,
Conceits and spells and vanishings
Where dragons crawl, and angels flap their wings.

Pastiche can seem a useful trick
And worth a moment's idle time,
A sort of rudimentary flick
Of parody and mucky rhyme
And therefore easy. So from slime
I rise to flaunt an obvious tale
And taunt the cruel with a crime
And read a lesson out in braille
And weigh a balance, and tip up the scale.

The Soldiers

The soldiers came over the hill. Some
Were crying, some were dragging legs
They could no longer carry.

One took a pick-axe out of his pocket
And broke the ice.

'Rum business.
There was a battle. But no-one knows where.

Actually, it took place in the air,
Most of it. The fall-out sawed the ground.

I was left with a cold in my joints
Nothing can cure.

He looks blind,
His eyelids won't open. But he can see,
Behind flesh.'

A third soldier said nothing
But went on counting the cost

On a pocket calculator
Until his hands fell off.

That was the first day of the war.

I Start with Spenser

I start with Spenser – well, why not?
And shorten him a foot or two.
It's like an illness I have got
And one I could pass on to you
With some reflections, like a view
Out of a mirror, into hell
Where Cocteau thought things looked quite blue.
Well, Dante may have done as well,
I reckon, if he could come back to tell.

But read it fast, it's doggerel stuff
And imitative, you may find,
Not often serious enough
And hardly fit to engage a mind
With geometry or Russia lined.
I offer it to those, a few
No doubt, who glance behind
Occasionally from the new
And wonder what was what, and who was who.

The Battle

We went to bed that night, listening for gunfire.
But, of course, we couldn't hear. We were too far away.
Or our ears were soundproof. Or they struck in silence.

Anyway, we slept, and woke to birdsong and frost
Over tarmac and field, in hollows and on the bark
And branches of all the trees. A warning of cold

Such as we rarely saw, an icing-up
Of whatever was normally fluid, in the first grip
Of a new winter, which would spread when the battle
                                                began.

To the Critic, Card-player and Mountaineer, A. Alvarez, Esq.

Alvarez, you've a level head
And ought to know a well-hung verse
If it's presented to you dead.
I wonder if you'll fret and curse
Or criticise me, and that's worse,
For offering so cold a thing
To your warm heart. With you as nurse
It can't lie there malingering
But must get up and try to sing
And generally act like fun.
Well, anyway, it may just swing
A little, and attempt to stun
With lines that move in Indian file,
As poker-faced, high-climbing style.

Envying the Submarine Commander

For Bill King

On certain days he saw the sun come up
Through a periscope, at nights the cats' eyes veer
Into tracer-shells. But it was no good.

They were amateurs, he and the Junkers,
Of a peace-time euphoria
Where sailing around the world
At sixty-three was a relaxation from hunting.

Nevertheless, he went up the conning-tower
Towards his eightieth birthday
And drew a bead on the *Graf Spee*,
Break-dancing.

The depth charges of arthritis were not for him.

Apology by an Ex-director

Life was a movie camera
Tracking through forests.

I used to pan over
Whole buildings
Just for fun.

Then tomorrow halved itself
And the fragment in short trousers
Ran to me, pleading for alms.

Noon was a head of steam once,
Breakfast used to race for the ankles,
But they buckled . . .

When I got up slowly,
The right hand in a cloud smiled grimly,
Unable to hold a tin-opener
Or masturbate.

I filmed a wheel-chair
In the distance, pirouetting in circles,
Catching the legs of flies.

Then everything stopped
Like God's breathing.

Now I sell stills.

In Memoriam

One day the great editor shot himself
In the leg. Nobody noticed
At first. The programmes came out for a while
Like normal. Good morning.
These are the minks. I speak Sham language.

Later, he had to limp with a stick
Towards the potentiometers. Hold your water,
A female comedienne shouted, from the Ladies'
Two floors below,
When he peed over the edge of the bowl.

At his funeral, soon after,
There were tinkers mungeing,
A few forgotten poets, and a girl friend
With long green hair, Miss Candida De'ath
Who had dogged him all his life.

They put the silver bullet
Called Syphilis
In his numbered coffin. But it wasn't, of course.
It was something worse. A neuropathic condition
For which there was never enough air-time
Called love of living.

Names

Those who have given their names
To dishes down the years
Form – like bananas – a bunch
A little frayed and yellow.

I think of Nectarine
(Piers Nectarine, remember?
You don't? Well, nor do I.
But Sandwich, yes? But Melba?)

Famous, though scarred, they mellow
Into a memory
Of much that must have mattered.
I tell you, I was shattered

When I discovered bleeney
Came from Mussolini,
A village in North Staffs.
It didn't? Well, you know

It might still get you laughs
Insisting that it did.
(Or Gwent, or Pontypridd.)
All origins of names

Are a gas for party games.
Think, much we eat was eaten,
And filmed, by Cecil Beaton.
Ayesha, Hore-Belisha

Beckon to us like beacons.
They stir a bud of taste
We mustn't let go waste.
She-soup? Sir Leslie's pudding?

Lord Abernethy – risk it –
Gave his name to a biscuit.
I christen my last breath
Soufflée MacBeth.

Remembering Making a School
Film at Symond's Yat

And is the dead dog buried still
They took across the railway-line
In 1950, George and John?

I wonder. But I scarcely care.
Too many other dogs have died
Since then, and lost their canine fur,

And left a legendary film
Of dust or celluloid or tears.
Nostalgia is in arrears.

Moreover, it could be that one
Way back would be to write of this
And lay the blame on something else

Like time or accidents or teeth
Not gritting like they ought. No way.
I see the mysteries grow sick

And vomit onto rugs of straw
Where able cats lie down and purr
And let the scout camp rot away

And Copley, and the other boys.
O, pets of presence! Pat your paws
And play with your too furious toys,

The Gulf War, and my failing nerve.
Some echo that might be applause
Shifts into Meadowhead, Broomhill

And Goodrich Castle, and the camp
Where all this happened has been struck
And no-one breathes there any more,

Not even Dawson, with his rushes.
Only the condoms and the thrushes
In their audition for a role

Upset the turf, surprise the mole.

Limitations

You can watch a species improving itself. Take
The pied wagtail, for example. They make

Their sudden swoops and dips, then run on wheels
Looking for food. It all feels

Awfully like an unpredictable success
For the colours of black and white. No stress

On anything beyond a swift movement of wings
And an accurate dive on tarmac. Things

Are looking up for a world in which a pied wagtail
Can find what it needs without fail

By using only speed and intelligence.
Limitations of this kind make sense.